Suzie sings, this is the color

Copyright © 2017 by Tomika Yvonne Reid

ISBN-13: 978-0-9975290-3-6

Library of Congress Control Number: 2020922752

Published by Tomika Reid

Printed in the United States of America 2020

Front Cover Design: Marc Poinson and Ron Comeau Designs

Back Cover Design: Marc Poinson

Dream big & Never give up. :)

Dedication

Parents, Teachers and Guardians, you are amazing for teaching our young ones.

Suzie is excited
about being in her
mother's backyard
skipping and singing
a song about the main colors.

"RED apples!" Suzie said, as she skipped around her mother's backyard.
[Singing] This is the color, this is the color, this is the color, RED.

Suzie continued to skip around
her mother's backyard.
"A BLUE ball!" Suzie, started singing.
[Singing] This is the color,
this is the color, this is the color,
BLUE.

Suzie enjoyed skipping, she then dropped her blue ball and saw a yellow sunflower! "YELLOW!" Suzie started to sing.
[Singing] This is the color, this is the color, this is the color,

Suzie ran to put the yellow sunflower on her mother's green table.

"GREEN table!" Suzie said, then she started to sing.
[Singing] This is the color, this is the color, this is the color,
GREEN.

Suzie had so much fun skipping
and singing in her mother's
backyard, it was where she spent
most of her time
playing.

"A BROWN bird!" Suzie laughed, pointing up to the bird near the apple tree. Suzie started to skip and sing. [Singing] This is the color, this is the color, this is the color, BROWN.

"Goodbye, brown bird!" Suzie says.

"Uh oh!" Suzie said, as she realized her shoelaces were untied.

Suzie sat on the green grass and tied her shoes the best way she knew how.

Suzie got up, and she saw a purple sand bucket. "PURPLE!" Suzie started to skip and sing. [Singing] This is the color, this is the color, this is the color, PURPLE.

Suzie skipped all around her mother's backyard, she had so much energy, and didn't show any sign of being tired. She continued to skip.

Suzie heard a loud sound, coming from the sky. "ORANGE airplane!" Suzie said, then she started to sing. [Singing] This is the color, this is the color, this is the color, ORANGE.

"Suzie, time to come in, wash up and get ready for supper!" Suzie's mom said, in a loud voice.

"Coming, mom." Suzie said, as she skipped her way into the
house, singing very excitedly.

"I know my colors mom, I know my colors. Go me!" Suzie was happy to know her colors.

When Suzie came in, to wash up for supper, she started to sing. [Singing] Red, Yellow, Brown, and Blue, Orange, Green, and Purple too! Suzie was happy, she knew her colors and had fun playing out in the backyard. [Singing] Red, Yellow, Brown, and Blue, Orange, Green, and Purple too! Red, Yellow, Brown, and Blue, Orange, Green, and Purple too!

Red

Blue

Orange

Purple

Yellow

Green

Brown

ENGLISH	SPANISH
Red	Rojo
Yellow	Amarillo
Green	Verde
Blue	Azul
Purple	Morado
Orange	Naranja
Brown	Marrón

The End!

Made in the USA
Middletown, DE
11 April 2022

63756840R00015